Managing Separation and Divorce

EMERALD GUIDES

Managing Separation and Divorce

Diane Roome & Elisabeth Sneade

Emerald Publishing
www.emeraldpublishing.co.uk

Emerald Guides
Brighton BN7 2SH

© Diane Roome and Elisabeth Sneade 2012

All rights reserved. No part of this publication may be reproduced in a retrieval system or transmitted by any means, electronic or mechanical, photocopying or otherwise, without the prior permission of the copyright holders.

ISBN 9781847162915

Printed by Berforts Press Herts

Cover design by Steve Swingler
Typesetting by wordzworth.com

Whilst every effort has been made to ensure that the information contained within this book is correct at the time of going to press, the author and publisher can take no responsibility for the errors or omissions contained within.

We would like to express our thanks to those colleagues (and clients) who have influenced us and motivated us to write this book. Our aim was to direct non-legally aware clients towards the help that they need. We hope that we have achieved this.

Diane profoundly thanks Lisa Birks for her unwavering help and support (and typing). We would both like to thank Caroline Lloyd-Evans for agreeing to write our introduction and providing encouragement.

Elisabeth would like to thank her parents for making it a little bit easier to return to work after two periods of maternity leave, and Neil for being a constant support. One day maybe Alicia and Isobel will read this and have a greater understanding of what is involved in being a family lawyer.

Contents

Introduction		**1**
Chapter 1	**Sorting Out the Emotional Stuff**	**3**
	It hurts where you are right now	3
	The potential costs if you don't	4
	Separation affects more than 2 people	5
	Can I do this on my own?	6
	Managing anger- Yours or your ex's	7
	Questionnaire	8
	Where to look for help	9
	Ten tips for effective communication with your ex	9
	Be prepared	11
	Main points from Chapter 1	13
Chapter 2	**Assessing What You Want to Achieve**	**15**
	Main points from Chapter 2	18
Chapter 3	**Finances**	**19**
	Immediate needs, paying the bills, assessing priority payments	19

	Housing	20
	Childcare	20
	Other debts	21
	Household bills	22
	Checklist for drawing up monthly budget	22
	Where to go for help with debt	24
	Information the professionals will need	25
	Main points from Chapter 3	27
Chapter 4	**Who the Professionals Are and What They Do**	**29**
	The lawyers	30
	The Financial Advisors (IFA's)	31
	Actuaries (aka the number geeks)	32
	Mediators	33
	Family counsellors	34
	Estate agents/surveyors	35
	General practitioner	36
	Accountants/tax specialist	37
	How to get the most from your lawyer and keep your costs down	38
	Start thinking about the future – take a structured approach	41
	Main points from Chapter Four	45

Chapter 5	**Dispute Resolution**	**47**
	Mediation or Collaborative Law?	48
	Mediation	49
	Collaborative Law	50
	How is mediation different to Collaborative Law?	51
	Family Arbitration	52
	Main points from Chapter 5	54
Chapter 6	**When to Spend Money on Professional Help**	**55**
	What can you do yourself?	55
	What if your case has complicated elements?	57
	How much can you DIY when it comes to agreeing the children's arrangements?	57
	What about the financial issues too?	58
	How do you approach DIY?	60
	So what bits is it best not to DIY?	65
	Main points from Chapter 6	66
Chapter 7	**Children**	**67**
	The effects of children's ages	68
	Talking to your children	70
	Parental alienation	70
	Telling the children	72

	Common questions children ask	73
	Main points from Chapter 7	75
Chapter 8	**Parenting Plan**	**77**
	Sample Parenting Plan	78
	Living arrangements	81
	Children's activities	82
	Travel	83
	Holidays	83
	Special days	84
	Phone calls	85
	House rules in each parents home	86
	Financial matters	87
	School / Education	89
	Communication	90
	Main points from Chapter 8	92
Chapter 9	**Moving on**	**93**
	The rules early on	93
	Get help if you need it	95
	Don't just talk – listen too	97
	Little people, little ears, long-term memories	98
	Beware of what you say online	99

What about the children?	99
Practical steps to take with the school	101
Kids' turn and talking to you	102
Key dates	103
Review	103
Main points from Chapter 9	105

Chapter 10 Resources — **107**

Summary of expenditure	107
Useful information	115
Useful websites and further information-general	118
Preparation questions	119

Recommended Reading	**121**
Index	**123**
Other Information	**125**

Introduction

Caroline Lloyd-Evans
Counsellor, Personal & Business Coach & Family Consultant

Separation and divorce are painful and difficult processes. The issues are emotional, psychological, financial, logistical and seemingly never-ending. They are certainly life-changing. Having supported numerous clients over two and a half decades through this quagmire, I have formed some strong opinions on the professionals – particularly the family lawyers – to whom clients turn for help and guidance. I've come to the conclusion that lawyers need three major attributes: a thorough and up-to-date knowledge of family law, a generous quantity of humanity and uncomplicated common sense. Surprisingly, one doesn't find that trio of qualities often enough, but I know from client feed-back that Elisabeth Sneade and Diane Roome demonstrate these essentials in their everyday practice.

This book also shows that they clearly possess these vital professional qualities in spades! In chapter 1 they ask that important question "Can I do it on my own?" They succinctly demonstrate that the minefield of concerns and problems facing the client, whichever party, can be carefully and sensitively worked through a good deal more smoothly and effectively if one is aware of the questions that need asking and the issues that are likely to arise.

Using this highly practical and logical book and getting help from other professionals such as counsellors and family consultants, decent and civilised compromises can be made which will benefit the couple, the children and the extended family.

Elisabeth and Diane quite rightly stress that keeping communication channels as open as possible between the couple and working towards consensus with the 'ex'-partner will be of tremendous benefit to the individuals, their children and the wider family for years to come. Great emphasis is placed on the plethora of problems concerning finances and the needs of the changing households which, if not handled properly, can be summed up by the phrase "fail to prepare and prepare to fail".

There are so many different routes that face clients when ending their relationships that it can seem like approaching a real 'spaghetti junction': collaboration, mediation, conciliation, litigation ... and these days, increasingly, DIY divorce with self-help books and the ever expanding 'expertise' on the internet. It is absolutely worth doing serious research before deciding which route to take and this includes getting help from the right source, experienced support from the best counsellor/family consultant, advice from a knowledgeable financial specialist, and direction and intelligent balanced legal counsel from the right family lawyer. If you're worrying and wondering which way to go, might I recommend you start here.

CAROLINE LLOYD-EVANS
CAMBRIDGE, UK
www.cleconsulting.co.uk

CHAPTER 1

Sorting Out the Emotional Stuff

It hurts where you are right now

When you separate from a partner, managing the emotional impact on you is a priority. Failure to address it can prove to be extremely costly in both financial and personal terms. However your separation came about, make no mistake; you will experience an emotional response. Don't be surprised as even if you separate on good terms you will still feel the effects of splitting from your partner.

We are not psychologists. The purpose of this chapter is to help you identify what is happening to you and to give consideration to seeking professional guidance to help you manage you, your feelings and the situation you find yourself in. We cannot change what has happened between you and your ex, but you can move forwards. It will take time and effort but can you do it!

You have a responsibility to yourself and your family, especially your children, to address your feelings about the split. Don't take this the wrong way. It is perfectly normal to experience a whole range of emotional responses when the decision to separate from a partner is made. The trick is to acknowledge that your feelings are a natural human response to the situation you are in, and then to deal with them, with or without professional help – that is up to you.

The potential costs if you don't

If you want to spend an hour in tears on the phone to your lawyer they will no doubt be extremely sympathetic BUT THEY WILL CHARGE YOU for that time! As this is likely to be a minimum of £150 then that is an extremely expensive phone call. You can do the maths – it won't take long to have a £1,000 plus bill if you spend time offloading your upset to your lawyer who will not be a therapist and therefore not able to help you with your feelings.

Then consider your friends and family. They will be kind, supportive and prepared to listen. But they can only do so much. Don't risk alienating them by passing on your distress to them for a long period of time. Even if you have a friend or relative with a professional qualification (e.g. psychologist, counsellor) we would suggest you consider seeing someone you don't know as the therapeutic relationship can then remain purely professional.

Separation affects more than 2 people

Think about your family and the people the split will affect. If we take a couple with 2 children and grandparents, then 8 people will be involved.

Children

Mum and Dad

Grandparents

Then there will be aunts, uncles and cousins. By this stage 20 people are in the affected group.

Aunts/Uncles

Cousins

Consider additional friends; say 3 couples, all of whom have 2 children. Then 12 more people are added to the group which by now totals 32 people.

Mum and Dad's friends

Mum and Dad's friend's children

We haven't even started to look at work colleagues, school friends and their parents. Some will be close to you and your ex, and they may be uncomfortable and worried about appearing to be disloyal to you or your ex. They will not want to 'take sides' and all we can say to you is it is up to you but if you have supportive and caring friends and family do you want to risk losing those relationships by forcing them to choose between you?

Can I do this on my own?

There are no right or wrong answers here. Be honest with yourself about how you feel and whether you are strong enough to deal with these feelings. There is absolutely no shame at all in admitting that you can't.

Try considering the following questions and then look at these answers to consider whether you want to seek additional help and support.

Managing anger- Yours or your ex's

Here are some tips for managing anger whether it's yours or your ex's.

- Get professional help if you need to
- Take responsibility for your part in the break-up
- Learn what pushes buttons – try to identify and understand what makes you angry
- Learn what pushes your ex's buttons – do you need to modify your own behaviour towards them?
- Be compassionate to both of you. What's happened has happened and can't be changed. Don't beat yourself or your ex up because it has.
- Be honest with yourself. If someone is angry with you, ask yourself why. Is there something in it?
- Don't be afraid to take a break and return to the discussion when things have calmed down.
- Don't take it personally- anger is a projection of one's feelings. It is their own turmoil which often leads to a person being angry.
- Forgive, let it go and move on. Do you want a future that is happy and fulfilled? Then let it go. Remember Catullus who wrote "I love and I hate. How can I do this you may ask? I don't, but it is excruciating and I am in hell"

Don't spend your life living like this. It's too short!

Questionnaire

This questionnaire is designed to help yourself identify whether you can effectively manage your emotions following your separation. If not, then could you benefit from some professional help?

1. How do I feel about myself?
    a) Am I distressed?
    b) Am I angry?
    c) Do I feel abandoned or rejected?
    d) Do I feel guilty?
    e) Do I blame them for the split?
    f) Do I blame myself for the split?
    g) Who do I feel is responsible for the separation?

2. How do I behave when I see and speak to my ex?
    a) Politely, with respect and objectively?
    b) Am I accusatory, angry and blaming them for what has happened?
    c) Can I speak to them clearly and convey my point with clarity?
    d) Am I very emotional and tearful?

3. Do I trust my ex
    a) With money?
    b) With the children's care and wellbeing?
    c) To be straightforward and honest with me

If you have answered 'yes' to any of the above questions we suggest that you seek additional help and support.

Where to look for help

Try your GP. They can signpost you or refer you to relevant services in your area.

British Association for Counselling & Psychotherapy
01455 883316
bacp@bacp.co.uk

Gingerbread
0808 802 0925

Relate
0300 100 1234

Ten tips for effective communication with your ex

1. Always be respectful. You loved each other once. If you have children they will always be the other parent. This is a situation you cannot change.

2. Keep your discussions factual. Use clear language without ambiguity. Ask direct questions e.g. "will you take the children to their swimming lesson on Saturday please?"

3. Do not start to apportion blame or look for answers you are unlikely to receive. For example, "why won't you ever take the children swimming?" or "you prefer to go to the match rather than take the children swimming," are unlikely to

produce a positive response and are much more likely to trigger an argument.

4. Do not have a detailed conversation when handing children over after a visit. Keep your conversation friendly and positive for the children's benefit.

5. When you need to have that detailed discussion make arrangements for:

    a) A mutually convenient time
    b) Set aside a neutral venue away from the family home if possible
    c) Set an agenda and remember you both have valid points to discuss
    d) Keep a note of any points agreed to avoid misunderstandings later on
    e) If this sounds like a business meeting then it might help to think of it this way

6. Do not worry if you do not agree with each other. That's life! If you were still together as a couple you would not agree on everything. It's ok to disagree but the trick is to manage disagreements and find a compromise or to agree to disagree.

7. Allow each other the opportunity to air your views. Don't shout each other down, and DO NOT swear or speak abusively to each other.

8. If you use email or text try not to be too curt as these methods of communication can be misunderstood as for example, a request can be interpreted as a demand!

9. Keep communication to the point you wish to address. Be specific.
10. Avoid discussing your ex on social networking sites. In our experience these discussions frequently find their way back to the subject of the 'chat'.

Not only does this lead to problems between adults but can impact negatively on children as their friends or their friends' parents may have seen and passed on the details.

Be prepared

There are various points during the separation process when you should be prepared to feel upset. The list below is by no means prescriptive, and we cannot guarantee there will not be other times when you will feel particularly emotional, but they do seem to be trigger factors common to many people.

1. When we receive any court papers, lets face it, to have something such as your personal relationship details set out formally and impersonally on court documents can be pretty chilling. The details may not look very pretty set down in black and white. Remember these documents are part of the process.
2. When looking at your financial position this may be uncomfortable. You are splitting one pot of money between you so measures such as downsizing your home or cutting back on regular expenditure may be necessary. Remember we can live without satellite TV or gym membership at least

for a while. Prioritise the essential spending and be prepared to consider cheaper alternatives to everything.

3. Telling the children, family and friends can be hard. If you can tell the child together with the other parent then not only does this mean you are supporting each other, but you are also sharing the responsibility. (There is more about how to tell the children in the chapter on children).

4. When you attend the formal meetings whether with your lawyer or mediator it is useful to take information with you in writing. (See the chapter on finances for a list of the information the lawyers will need).

Now read the main points from Chapter 1 overleaf.

Main points from Chapter 1
Sorting Out the Emotional Stuff

1. When you separate from a partner, managing the emotional impact on you, and others, is a priority. Failure to address it can prove extremely costly in both personal and financial terms.

2. Separation affects more than 2 people-think about your family and the people the split will affect.

3. There are a number of places where you can look for help-your GP, Counsellors, Relate and others.

4. Be prepared-there are various points along the separation process where you should be prepared to feel upset.

CHAPTER 2

Assessing What You Want to Achieve

Once you are sure your relationship is over it is well worthwhile taking stock of what you want to achieve.

The key question to ask yourself at the outset is "what would I do if I was in my ex's shoes?" The sooner you are able to do this, the sooner you will be able to enter into negotiations positively and arrive at a mutually acceptable solution.

There are a number of 'deadly' obstacles to negotiation which are not too far removed from the deadly sins! Don't let any of these apply to you as they are likely to incur significant emotional and financial costs!

- Anger will simply waste time and energy.
- Jealousy will be counterproductive, get you nowhere and remember you are no longer in a relationship with the other person.

MANAGING SEPARATION AND DIVORCE

- Greed makes any form of reasonable negotiation impossible.
- Pride results in statements. Let go of your principles and be practical.
- Lust will just get in the way- if its well and truly over stay focused on sorting out solutions.
- Fear can be the worst enemy of productive negotiations.
- Separation and divorce is a very difficult time and fear of the unknown can be a very effective blocker to moving on.

Remember there are options for both of you. Focus on the problem, not the person. Be practical and realistic- you may have loved the family home but if you can't afford it on your own is it realistic to stay there? It is the people who make a home – if you've built one you can build another.

Ask yourself some questions before you start any form of negotiation.

1. List 5 things you want to get out of mediation / collaboration/negotiation and why you have listed them.
2. List 5 things you think the other person wants to get out of the process and why.
3. What are your 5 greatest worries and why are they of concern.
4. What do you think the other persons 5 greatest worries are and why?
5. What are your goals for yourself and your children at the conclusion of the process?

ASSESSING WHAT YOU WANT TO ACHIEVE

6. Work out for yourself, with your answers to the previous questions in mind the following:
   a) The most you would be willing to give or give up
   b) The least you would be willing to give or give up
   c) The bottom line you would be willing to agree upon

7. Do some homework. Look at the alternative costs of housing – e.g. mortgage costs or monthly rental costs and have a look at some other properties. It can be a useful exercise if only to rule out some options as unaffordable.

8. Avoid treating everything as of equal importance. Don't get hung up over the last 5 glasses in the cupboard.

9. Is there a solution you can live with?

   THINK   'acceptable' not 'fair'
                   'how' not 'why'
                   'problem' not 'person'
                   'achievable' not 'principle'

Now read the main points from Chapter 2 overleaf.

Main points from Chapter 2
Assessing What You Want to Achieve

1. Once you are sure your relationship is over, it is well worthwhile taking stock of what you want to achieve.

2. There are a number of "deadly obstacles" to negotiation - but don't let them apply to you, as they are likely to incur significant emotional and financial costs.

CHAPTER 3

Finances

Immediate needs, paying the bills, assessing priority payments

One of the first issues to think about when separating is to agree who is going to pay the bills and which must be paid immediately to avoid further problems developing at a later date. If you can agree at the outset who will pay the bills it will then give you both time to breath and then identify what you would like to achieve long term. If you cannot agree who is going to pay the mortgage then you will very quickly find yourself dealing with red letters arriving in the post and that only adds to what is already a stressful situation. The more non-payment of bills takes place the fewer options you will find available to you in terms of credit being offered which could then take away your preferred financial settlement. If you are thinking in terms of you or your spouse taking on the current mortgage rather than selling the house for goodness sake prioritise payment of the mortgage otherwise you may find that you are considered a 'bad risk'. So what are the important bills to be paid? Each case will vary but listed below are the top priorities in most cases.

Housing

Who is going to pay the mortgage or rent?

Will you pay half each or will one of you pay this and the other pay for something else? Much will depend on whether you are both going to stay living in the house until you have reached an agreement about finances. If one of you is moving out it will probably be the case that the person staying at the house will pay the mortgage or rent.

There may be help available to you in the short term. Think about talking to your lender about arranging a mortgage holiday to give yourself some breathing space, but remember this could affect your credit rating. Perhaps your lender will agree to you switching to an interest only mortgage for a short time.

Wherever you live, and it sounds obvious, make sure that you prioritise paying for your home! If you are in rented accommodation you may qualify for state benefits to help you meet the cost of your rent.

Childcare

If you both work and are going to keep working how will you pay for childcare?

If you are separated from your spouse or partner you may now qualify for state benefits (tax credits) to help reduce the cost of childcare. Many parents find that the cost of childcare is a large percentage of one parent's income. When you separate the parent with whom the children live may find that once they have paid for childcare there is nothing left to pay for the mortgage or rent, let alone buy food and pay all of the other day-to-day bills. Try to agree early on how this cost will be met, particularly if both of you are going to continue working. Also give consideration to how childcare costs during the school holidays will be paid. When one parent works school hours the need for childcare is often largely out of sight as it tends to be only at Easter, Christmas and the summer holidays that this cost becomes a problem. Can family members or friends help out, or do you have enough holidays between the two of you to cover this time with the children? Perhaps there is a holiday club that could provide the childcare that you need?

Other debts

Other debts such as credit cards, car finances, unsecured loans

Most of us will owe money, other than for our mortgage, in a variety of forms whether that be a car loan, a home improvement loan to do up the kitchen or some other house-based project, or money spent on our credit cards for those items we wanted but didn't have the cash at the time to afford. It is not unusual for clients to meet with their lawyers and have in excess of £10k owing on credit cards plus other loans too. Very often if you are meeting the loan repayments comfortably out of your joint income is easy to forget what a drain on individual finances these payments can be.

It is often not until couples separate that the repayments become an issue. If you find that making the monthly payments is going to be tricky when you separate, be upfront with your creditors. They would much prefer to receive the money you owe over more months, than you default. Keep your creditors in the loop and make minimum payments if necessary. If you miss payments it will affect your credit rating and may make it more difficult to secure other financing later on.

Household bills

It is easy to miss the different expenses involved in running a household. It is often not until you have to face meeting those costs out of a sole income having paid for them jointly that you realise how many different bills there are to pay. Write a list and decide which of your current expenses you need to continue to have. Is it vital, for example, that you have the all-singing-all-dancing Sky package? Could you have Freeview instead? Think of the costs involved and whether you can continue your current lifestyle. Two incomes to run one household is very a different proposition!

Checklist for drawing up monthly budget

Where do you start? Prepare a monthly budget to see what your costs are. Look at the Summary of Expenditure in the Appendix for an example. Separate your costs out into:-

- Housing
- Car running costs
- Domestic expenses
- Personal expenses

- Replacement items
- Costs associated with your children

Next, be honest with yourself. If you are spending beyond your means take decisive action to cut your costs. Change your shopping habits, use online resources to get better deals from your utility providers and cut down on the frivolous spending. Do you really need a coffee each lunch time? Could you use that £10 in a more constructive way? Make the most of the online voucher schemes and comparison websites.

Although it is rather time-consuming and rather dull to sit and work out your budget shortly after your separation if you prioritise this you will save time and money in the long run. One of the first things your lawyer is going to need to know from you is what are the priority bills that need to be paid and who is going to pay them? In addition, the information contained in the mass of paperwork you will sift through when putting together your budget is not lost time. The information will be needed by the other professionals, such as financial advisors, throughout your case.

Remember that the best way to reduce your legal and other costs is to be organised and provide the information asked for by your representatives swiftly. If you have already agreed your budget and worked out how your monthly expenses are going to be met when you separate into two households you will have saved a great deal of time and therefore money.

Where to go for help with debt

There are many organisation that offer help to those who are struggling to pay their debts. Being upfront with those that you owe money to is the priority. The CAB offer debt advice as do many charities. The Government advice website *www.direct.gov.uk* is also particularly useful and user-friendly. Try to avoid, if you can, debt management companies who charge an administration fee for dealing with your debts as that may well add to your money worries rather than help. The Money Advice Service *www.moneyadviceservice.org.uk* is government based but established in conjunction with a leading family lawyer and is another useful resource.

Many mortgage companies are willing to consider a 'mortgage holiday' period which means you pay a reduced rate for 6 months or so. This may give you and your former partner time to agree what is going to happen long term to the family home and reach a long-term settlement. If you try to reach a quick agreement because both of you are very aware that you only have enough money to pay the next 2 months' mortgage you will often feel resentful later on that you rushed into those decisions. See if you can 'restructure' your debt. For example, could you consolidate several outstanding credit card debts into one loan that is easier to manage? Make sure that you are always paying off the debt with the highest rate of interest first as your priority (in addition to paying your housing costs) and then work your way down your list to the next highest interest paying debt and so on.

FINANCES

Information the professionals will need

Using a checklist based on court statements will save time later on

In addition to a completed summary of expenditure the professionals involved in your case whether they be lawyers, financial advisors or someone else are all going to want to see similar documentation. If you gather everything together at the outset you will help yourself get the advice you need as soon as possible. You will also save time as the professionals will not have to wait to advise you about a particular issue until they have all of your information to hand.

What will they need?

1. A valuation of the family home or confirmation of your current tenancy agreement
2. Your most recent mortgage statement
3. Your last 6 month wage slips together with your P60 and P11D, (if you have one)
4. Copies of bank statements for the last 12 months for *each* bank account
5. If you run your own business copies of your most recent profit and loss accounts (if possible covering the past 2 years)
6. Details of any state benefits you receive
7. A list of the other assets you have such as endowment policies, savings, shares
8. A list of the other liabilities you have such as unsecured loans and credit cards

9. Your most recent pension statement
10. Confirmation of your mortgage capacity
11. Details of alternative housing options on a purchase and rental basis together with any special requirements such as a map showing school catchment areas.

Now read the main points from Chapter 3 overleaf.

Main points from Chapter 3
Finances

1. One of the first issues to think about when separating is to agree who is going to pay the bills and which ones must be paid immediately.
2. If you can agree at the outset who is going to pay the bills, it will give you both time to breathe and plan for the longer term.
3. It is very important to prioritise the bills-for example housing and childcare payments.
4. Prepare a monthly budget so you can see clearly what your costs are.
5. If you are struggling to pay debts, there are many organisations in existence that offer help and advice.

CHAPTER 4

Who the Professionals Are and What They Do

When you instruct a lawyer very often you think that you will be the only one to deal with them. Whilst many years ago that was certainly the case nowadays lawyers work closely with a range of other professionals to offer their clients the best service to meet their individual needs. The professionals most commonly used are:-

1. The lawyers
2. Financial advisors
3. Actuaries
4. Mediators
5. Family counsellors
6. Estate agents
7. GPs
8. Accountants/Tax specialists

The lawyers

Your lawyer will always be your first point of call. It is the lawyer who is instructed by you to resolve your divorce and/or financial issues following your separation. A good lawyer will identify early on where other professionals will be needed and delegate specific tasks within your case to them at relevant points. Your lawyer can provide you with all of the legal advice but they cannot and must not advise you about other issues outside the area of their expertise. For example, your lawyer cannot tell you what your mortgage capacity is going to be or calculate how much of your pension you should transfer to your husband or wife. These tasks must be delegated to the specialists.

Your lawyer may work on a fixed-fee or per-hour basis. Be clear at the outset what is and is not covered in their costs. Will you have to pay to speak to their secretary or not? How much money do they want from you 'up front'? Can you pay monthly or set up a standing order and if you pay by credit card are you charged extra to do this? How much will you be charged for photocopying? Most financial statements are 100+ pages long.

Until recently, many firms would agree that a client could pay their legal costs when the family home is sold meaning your lawyers waited to be paid until the end of your case. Nowadays it is rare for law firms to do this. 'Cash is King' in the legal business meaning that many firms will bill you monthly and say that if invoices are unpaid for more than a month no further work will be done on your case. You may also be charged interest on any outstanding balance.

Where do you find your lawyer? Personal recommendation is always a good idea. If someone has acted for a friend or family member and they did a good job you will be more inclined to use them than an unknown person. Many family lawyers are members of Resolution and you can search their website for lawyers in your local area (*www.resolution.org.uk*). If a lawyer is a member of Resolution it means that they will abide by the Resolution Code of Conduct so that negotiations are carried out in as non-confrontational way possible.

Your needs as the client are prioritised over sending vitriolic letters. More importantly, it is recognised that where there are children involved, their needs will be at the centre of all discussions. The Citizens Advice Bureaux often have lists of local lawyers and a comparison of their various charges.

The Financial Advisors (IFA's)

Most people will know of a financial advisor who has helped a friend or family member but many people do not have a designated IFA. Lawyers will have good links with the local financial advisors and should be able to recommend several in your area who can help.

Why do you need a financial advisor? Not all clients do. Most people come into contact with IFAs when setting up a pension, sorting out life insurance or managing your investments. Some IFA's are now specially trained in family law to enable them to better work alongside family lawyers. This means that they have an understanding of how the law works and a view of how the Court would treat your case if it went to a contested hearing. Resolution has set a detailed exam which those IFAs who want to be seen as a 'divorce specialist' are able to take. Details of IFA's who have the experience to give advice on family cases can be found on the Resolution website.

Your lawyer will probably ask you to meet with an IFA if you are thinking about having your former partner's pension transferred in part to you or vice versa. The IFA will be able to explain how much money you are likely to receive after a transfer takes place.

Another less well-known function that a financial advisor can perform is helping to bring people quickly up to speed with their finances. Very often one half of the couple has been charged with 'dealing with the money'. This tends to mean the other person has little or no clue about what money is where, or even who their mortgage company is. An IFA will quickly be able to bring that person up to speed and answer any questions they have so that they are then confident to firstly, tell their lawyer what they want to achieve, and secondly, do not feel like they are unclear when discussing financial issues with their former partner. Knowledge is power as they say!

Actuaries (aka the number geeks)

Most people have pensions and, when they separate, those pensions remain a matrimonial asset that is divided just as the equity in a house or money in a bank account. The difference is that a pension is invested for a number of years and is often linked to the stock market making it very difficult to predict how much it is worth now and in a number of years ahead.

When dealing with pensions there tends to be three approaches.

1. You can decide that you both keep your own pensions and other assets may be offset to deal with any in-balance in your pension provision.

2. Alternatively, you can equalise pensions meaning that you both have the same amount invested in your pensions following your divorce.

3. Lastly, you can equalise income on retirement.

A lawyer cannot do the complicated calculation to work out how much of one pension should be transferred to another person in order to equalise pensions. That is the role of an actuary.

Complicated factors such as your respective ages, health factors and the specific pension investments that you each have are relevant factors. Actuaries tend to be instructed jointly so that you both share in the cost of paying for their advice. It may feel like you are paying a lot of money for a calculation to be carried out and to some extent this is true. However, over a number or years the difference between 1% and 2% of pension can make a real difference when planning for your retirement.

There are many actuaries who specialise in doing the specialist calculations with pensions in divorce cases. Your lawyer should be able to tell you who to instruct and give you an idea of likely cost.

Mediators

Mediators act as an impartial third party between you and your ex to facilitate your discussions in trying to reach consensus between you. Mediation is not compulsory, although is a requirement that before anyone makes an application to Court that a referral to mediation is made. It may be that you have dealings with a Mediator on an assessment basis who then decides that you and your former partner do need the Court to help you resolve your disputes.

Other couples though find Mediation a useful venue to resolve their disputes. The idea of Mediation is that you and your former partner are able to negotiate towards a final agreement (whether that be in terms of your financial issues or children's arrangements) with the mediator being the neutral third party keeping things as calm as possible and on-track towards a negotiated settlement.

A mediator works alongside your lawyer as although they may be a lawyer, not all mediators are. Mediators are able to tell you the sort of settlements that a Court would accept but they cannot go into detail about whether a particular proposal is the right one for you to accept. That remains the role of your lawyer. As a way of resolving your disputes mediation is competitive in terms of cost and time as not only do mediators tend to charge less per hour than your respective lawyers, they are able to have meetings as and when it suits you and your former partner. For example, if you both agree you want to meet every week until you have an agreement there is nothing to stop you doing so.

Family counsellors

Frequently as lawyers our clients will talk to us about issues that are not strictly part of their legal proceedings but nevertheless have an impact on how they conduct their day-to-day lives. Separating from your partner is an incredibly emotional time and having the right support in place will help you both adjust to your new situation. Family counsellors are trained to offer the emotional support that your lawyer cannot provide.

child's school to arrange counselling for them if required, they can ensure both parents are kept informed if you have a child who regularly requires medical treatments by making sure the other parent who does not attend with your child at the surgery receives a letter confirming the treatment agreed. Very often, the act of your GP ensuring that the other parent is kept informed will ensure that arguments are stopped before they start. Prior to your separation the discussions of what happened at the GPs would have taken place at home, but if you are separated or finding it difficult to communicate this action by your GP can be incredibly helpful.

From time to time we, as lawyers, have clients who fail to cope with the emotional impact of a relationship breakdown. Their ability to provide clear instructions to the lawyer becomes impaired. If your GP is proactive and willing to liaise with your lawyer to potentially appoint someone else to make decisions whilst you are unable to do so it saves time and money. If you have a friend or family member who you think perhaps should not be making decisions about their legal issues get them to discuss this with their GP.

Accountants/tax specialist

Not every case requires the involvement of an accountant or tax specialist. As with family counsellors, your lawyer should be able to identify when outside help is required and refer you to that specialist as soon as possible. If you run your own business or perhaps your former partner has complicated business dealings the involvement of their business accountant may be required to explain how the money within the business works and whether it is possible to borrow against the business to fund your new lives.

If you are suspicious that your former partner is not disclosing all that they should be within your financial negotiations you may be asked to consider appointing a forensic accountant. A forensic accountant specialises in analysing, interpreting and summarising complication financial and business related issued in a way that is understandable and properly supported with evidence. In much the same way that Actuaries are considered the 'pension geeks', forensic accountants are the 'number geeks'! Your lawyer will not be qualified to advise you about the complicated nature of someone's business accounts but they should be able to spot when outside help is required. If you think your lawyer is getting out of their depth or you don't fully understand the explanations you are being given ask them for an expert to be appointed to clarify the situation.

How to get the most from your lawyer and keep your costs down

Ask any client who comes for a first meeting with their lawyer and their priorities will be to obtain the best advice for their particular situation without paying excessive legal bills. Listed below are some practical ways that you can ensure you keep your legal costs under control and at the same time get the most from the lawyer you instruct.

- Before your first meeting make a note of the key points you want to discuss and give the note to your lawyer at the start of your meeting, or better still, email it to them beforehand.

- Avoid lengthy telephone calls when you could perhaps be more succinct in an email or letter. Remember your lawyer will charge for all the time spent working on your case.

WHO THE PROFESSIONALS ARE AND WHAT THEY DO

- Try to avoid using your lawyer to provide emotional support. Lawyers are good but expensive listeners. Use your lawyers to provide the legal advice and obtain emotional support from your GP or meet with a family counsellor.

- Be organised. Take a pen and note pad to your meeting. If your lawyer tells you to obtain a list of documents get them to your lawyer ASAP. Every time they chase you for some outstanding information you will be charged!

- Keep all of your documents regarding your case in a file so that you have them in one place. By the end of your case you may have received lots of correspondence and often re-reading the past few letters sent between all involved prior to a meeting will refresh your memory and perhaps answer some of the questions you have.

- Ask upfront what you can do yourself and which bits you need your lawyer to do. If you are confident at form-filling perhaps you could do the paperwork associated with applying for the divorce and ask your lawyer to concentrate on reaching a financial agreement. This could save you an average of £600!

- Be clear at the beginning what your legal costs budget is for and apportion your money accordingly. Don't instruct expensive experts if you cannot afford them! If experts are required make sure you agree with your former partner how they are going to be paid.

- Ask your lawyer where junior members of their team can help. Often lawyers will have trainees who charge less per hour but will be fully able to prepare straightforward court documents. Often a trainee is half the cost of your lawyer.

- If you have to attend Court discuss with your lawyer whether it is more cost effective for a barrister to attend with you. Factor in the time your lawyer will spend waiting with you at court against a fixed fee that can be agreed for a barrister to attend with you. Remember that your lawyer should have good relationships with your local barristers' chambers and if money is short don't be too embarrassed to ask your lawyer to see if the barristers can 'do you a deal'!

- Utilise your lawyer's assistant/secretary. They work closely alongside your lawyer and if you have a straightforward question more times than not they will be able to answer it for you. You will probably find that there is no charge for this whereas if you speak to your lawyer you will be charged!

- When providing documents to your lawyer for financial disclosure ask how many copies they will need. Many law firms charge you for photocopying and this can be a hidden cost until you see you monthly invoice. It is not uncommon for a photocopying bill to be £20+ if you are sending a lengthy financial statement to the Court. It is often cheaper for you to print off additional copies direct from your online banking if you have this facility.

- Ask your lawyers what fixed fees they offer and what online packages are available. More and more law firms are turning to fixed price work especially for the less complicated tasks such as divorce. Some firms also offer an online service where you are asked a series of questions, your forms are then generated and checked by a member of the family team before you send them to the Court yourself.

- Ask your lawyer what other charges will be incurred. Will your lawyer obtain documents from the Land Registry as a matter of routine to establish ownership of your family home, or do they liaise with their property colleagues who may be instructed to sell your home and get copies from them?

Start thinking about the future – take a structured approach

Deciding what you want from your new life is not an easy question to answer. Some elements may be fairly obvious in that you may want to remain living in the same area as where your children attend school or you have family and friends nearby to provide support, both emotional and practical. Other issues may not be immediately clear as you might prefer to stay living at the family home but finances prevent that from happening. However difficult it is to face unhappy truths, such as you cannot afford a mortgage the size of your current one, the earlier you accept those issues the easier it will be for you to focus on your future.

Each family case is different and no two outcomes are ever the same. It used to be that the bane of a family lawyer's life was the 'advice down the pub' that their client received. More commonly now it is the information they have seen on the 'web' that is going to colour a person's view of the outcome they expect. Managing your expectations should be handled sensitively by your lawyer. If what you are seeking to achieve is not possible you should be told this as soon as possible otherwise you will put plans in place to achieve your long-term goal and be very disappointed when it becomes apparent that they cannot be reached.

Listed below are some things for you to think about. Some answers will be easy but others will take time for you to come to a considered decision.

- Where would you like to live? Would you prefer to remain living in the family home or is it more practical for financial reasons to relocate or downsize?

- If you are going to move, what alternative housing do you need? Draw up a list of things that you 'need' such as staying within your child's current school catchment area, and things that are 'preferred', such as off road parking or a sizeable garden.

- Is renting a more practical short-term option if it means you can sell the family home and reduce your debts?

- Will work change if you are separating? Do you need to change your working pattern to accommodate your children where before you and your former partner shared the pre and after school care? Can family members or friends help out with the practical arrangements in the short and longer term?

- What outside help do you need? If you are not financially aware is it worth meeting with an IFA to have your current financial situation clarified so you can make informed decision? Get 'money-smart'.

WHO THE PROFESSIONALS ARE AND WHAT THEY DO

- What about your long-term financial security? Providing housing now and an income to meet your day-to-day needs is important but so is provision for your retirement. Does this need to be addressed as part of your overall discussions or do you both agree you are relatively young and able to make provision for yourselves?

- Have you made a new Will? What happens if either of you died before a final agreement is reached, would you want your former partner to inherit? If not, make a new Will!

- Do you need to close joint bank accounts? If one of you is moving out of the family home and moving into rented housing whilst you sort out the long-term arrangements it will probably be easier to close all joint accounts so that one of you is not concerned about the other potentially going overdrawn.

- Does one of you need interim maintenance? Are the day-to day expenses going to be met from individual income or is there a shortfall? Prioritise the bills that need paying and consider those expenses which can be cut for the time being.

- If you are both going to stay living in the family home until it is sold consider the practical arrangements. How will you feel if your former partner brings a new partner to the house? What are you going to do about the household chores? Are you going to agree who does the cooking, cleaning etc. or are you going to employ a cleaner instead?

- What arrangements need to be put in place to provide security for your children? How often will they see each parent? Do the children need emotional support from outside the family home?

This is by no means an exhaustive list and just a starting point. The ideal is that you and your former partner are able to agree together how you will resolve your differences and how you will manage your separation. Not all couples are able to do so without the involvement of lawyers and perhaps other professionals. The reality is that just because you are pragmatic and approach matters in the most sensible way possible there is no guarantee that your former partner will do so and for some cases court hearings and costly litigation will be inevitable.

Having advised many clients over the years our suggestion is that you look at the 'preparation questions' in the Appendix and try to answer them as honestly as you can. By all means ask your former partner to do the same. At its worst you will identify areas that you disagree but at its best you will be able to focus on the same goals. A frequently chosen goal among clients is the idea that when your children marry or graduate you would like to be able to both be there to support them. How you manage your divorce and the emotions that form part of that separation will be the biggest single factor that determines whether or not that is possible.

You will have probably attended many social events where friends have only been able to invite their Mum or Dad for fear that if both parents are present there will be an 'atmosphere'. Is this what you want for your children? Probably not! Have that as your goal when everything seems to be too much to cope with and you won't go too far wrong in our opinion.

Now read the main points from Chapter 4 overleaf.

Main points from Chapter Four
Who the Professionals are and What They Do

1. There are a number of professionals involved when going through a divorce, you will need to consider carefully which ones you are likely to need.

2. A lawyer will usually be the first port of call and a good lawyer will identify early on where the professionals will be needed.

3. Be clear at the outset what your lawyer covers ion their costs and what is not included.

4. Many family lawyers are members of Resolution and you can search their website for lawyers in your location.

5. Start thinking now about what will happen in the future. Don't leave it until it gets messy and complicated.

CHAPTER 5

Dispute Resolution

Dispute resolution (or ADR "alternative dispute resolution" as it is often called) is a process whereby you and your ex work through your case with the help of either a mediator or collaborative lawyers. The aim is to come up with solutions everyone can live with and draw up a detailed settlement which can be incorporated into a Court Order if appropriate. There are a number of potential benefits for you and your family if you can settle matters between you using one of the dispute resolution processes:-

- You can maintain civil working relationships by taking your issues out of the adversarial court arena. If you are parents you will see each other for years to come, so far better for yourselves and the children if you can work together to ensure those relationships are not yet destroyed.

- You remain in control of the decisions. If you go to Court you are effectively saying to the Judge "we can't agree, so you decide'

That is precisely what the Judge will do. Their decision may not be what either of you want.

- Time saving. You can expect the Court process to take at least 6 months. With dispute resolution you are part of managing the timescale.

- Flexibility. It is far easier to rearrange a dispute resolution appointment than a Court Hearing (although we would not encourage frequent changes as that can be indicative of a lack of commitment to participate in the process). You can ask for a break in the session.

- Costs savings. Dispute resolution is a considerably cheaper option than either negotiating through lawyers and/or going to court.

- Incorporating Additional Support. Dispute resolution processes can utilise where necessary referrals to other professions such as Financial Advisors, Actuaries and Counsellors.

Mediation or Collaborative Law?

There are two main types of family dispute resolution currently practised. Mediation involves commonly a single mediator, although sometimes two mediators will work together. This is known as co – mediation. Collaborative law involves a series of round-the-table meetings between you and your ex with both lawyers present.

Mediation

Usually, a series of meetings take place between you and your ex and a mediator. The mediator's job is to put a structure to your discussions, to remain neutral, and to help you arrive at a set of proposals you can both live with. You will find that negotiations relating to both children and finances will be conducted parallel to each other, so you can expect to address both areas during each session. Sessions commonly last for no more than 1-1 ½ hours.

Three mediation sessions is about average, but there are no rules as to how many sessions are required. That is down to you and your mediator.

Expect to have "homework", particularly in relation to financial information. Your mediator is likely to ask you to collate details of your current financial position and to consider issues such as where you propose to live in the future.

You will need to look at the affordability of your proposals. Sometimes it can be worth considering various options if only to rule some out as being unfeasible.

You have the scope to test out some proposals, say, the children's arrangements. If a particular element doesn't work you are free to discuss it again during the next session.

Dispute Resolution involves a series of "steps". You may need to "tweak" your initial suggestions. There is absolutely nothing wrong with this – far better to resolve the problem at an early stage when you have professional support from your mediator and/or lawyer.

You can retain the services of your own lawyer throughout mediation if you wish. Indeed, mediators regularly encourage those in mediation to take their known legal advice at various stages.

A mediator cannot advise the participants in mediation. Occasionally a mediation session will take place with both lawyers present, but only if necessary as paying the costs of three professionals can provide expensive!

At the end of mediation a summary of your proposals is incorporated into what is known as a "Memorandum of Understanding". In England and Wales this document is not legally binding in itself. However it is usually incorporated into a Court Order drafted by the lawyers which can be sent for a Judge's approval without your having to turn up at Court.

Collaborative Law

The collaborative process is very similar to mediation in that the aim is to assist you to resolve issues arising from your separation in a dignified and respectful way for the benefit of the whole family. It is a slightly different process to mediation.

- You and your partner retain separate, specially trained lawyers, who will assist you to resolve issues without going to court.

- Your collaborative lawyer will provide you with the advice required but will also work with your partner and their lawyer as part of a team to help reach an agreed settlement.

- You, your partner, and your lawyers agree to work together in a respectful, honest and dignified way without threatening to go to court.

- You sign an agreement disqualifying your collaborative lawyer from representing you at court if the process breaks down. Neither of the lawyers, or their respective firms, can represent you.

- Issues are discussed and hopefully resolved in a series of 'four-way' face-to-face meetings between you, your lawyer, your partner and their lawyer. Settlement discussions take place in your presence which helps to ensure that you and your partner remain in charge of the process. This process helps communication and is particularly important when you have children.

How is mediation different to Collaborative Law?

- In mediation, the mediator is prohibited from giving you legal advice, and cannot assist you in advocating a position. The mediator remains neutral.

- A mediator has a duty to advise you both to take separate legal advice. This is not necessary in collaborative law as your lawyer is present with you at any discussion.

- Any settlement discussed at mediation is only binding upon you once you have each had the opportunity to take your own legal advice and have transferred the agreement into a separation consent order of the court. The mediator cannot produce the court documents for you, nor finalise the process.

- Provided it is agreed, your collaborative lawyer can act for you in the divorce and prepare the court papers to obtain the consent order.

- Lawyers are rarely present during the mediation sessions, and their advice may be given too late to assist in the process. With collaborative law you receive the legal advice at the time the issue is raised.

Collaborative law is not suitable for every client, or indeed every lawyer, but it is worth considering as an alternative to mediation.

Family Arbitration

Arbitration is another form of dispute resolution recently developed to deal with financial and property issue in family disputes (It has been a method utilised to resolve commercial and contact disputes for some time). The parties enter into an agreement whereby they appoint a qualified arbitrator to adjudicate their dispute and produce a binding result. The arbitrator effectively acts as a private judge and it is an option for couples who want to resolve financial disputes quickly without a court hearing.

Arbitration cannot be used where one party is bankrupt or insolvent, nor can it be used in disputes dealing with the care and /or parenting of children. In most cases there will be a preliminary meeting and a Final Hearing if matters cannot be agreed, but arbitration can be conducted in its entirety as a paper exercise. A final decision made by an Arbitrator is known as an award.

There are a number of potential advantages when comparing arbitration to Court process in that the parties can choose their arbitrator; the timeline is decided by the participants; the entire process is confidential and it is likely there will be a substantial saving of costs when compared to expensive court proceedings. At present there are no more than 35 qualified arbitrators but this is expected to be a growth area.

Now read the main points from Chapter 5 overleaf.

Main points from Chapter 5
Dispute Resolution

1. Dispute Resolution (ADR) is a process whereby you and your ex works through your case with the help of a mediator or a collaborative lawyer.

2. The main aim of dispute resolution is to come up with solutions everyone can live with and draw up a detailed settlement.

3. Mediation is distinct from collaborative law. In mediation, the mediator is prohibited from giving legal advice where this isn't the case where lawyers are involved.

4. Family arbitration is another form of dispute resolution recently developed to deal with financial and property affairs arising in family disputes.

CHAPTER 6

When to Spend Money on Professional Help

What can you do yourself?

Form-filling and online options

It used to be considered the norm that when your relationship broke down you made an appointment to meet with a solicitor and instructed them to 'sort' the issues. By that we mean apply to the court for your divorce (liaising with your former partner beforehand on the best way to achieve that) and then negotiate either directly with your former partner or their solicitor to agree the financial arrangements and practical arrangements for your children. Technology combined with the need for families to reign in their outgoings when the cost of everything around them is increasing has meant that is no longer the norm.

In 2001 when we first qualified it was unusual for clients to be dealing directly with the court and filling out their own paperwork to apply for a divorce. Public funding was freely available to assist with the cost of the divorce process and if you were paying privately it was considered the norm for your lawyer to deal with this for you. The proliferation of the internet coupled with the drastic reduction in available public funding has lead to a massive change in this process in the past 10 years.

There is a myriad of information available telling you how to apply for a divorce, together with online examples of how the forms should be completed. There are forums to discuss the best way to proceed with your case and even Her Majesty's Court Service have grasped the importance of modern technology and made their website fairly user-friendly.

It is now unusual for us as lawyers to be asked to prepare the Divorce Petition as this is a key way that clients see they can take control of their process and save money at the same time. With court fees to obtain a divorce now at £385 (current as of autumn 2011) it is easy to see why clients don't then want to spend a further £600 paying for their lawyer to complete forms that they feel able to do themselves.

Some law firms have moved with the times and embraced the concept of client-led services with online form packages available through their websites or offering fixed-fee divorces. The benefit of both of these to you as the client is that you keep your costs under control but still retain the involvement of your lawyer either at a minimal level, if it is an online forms package, or at an agreed costs level, if you have a fixed- fee agreement.

What if your case has complicated elements?

The difficulty for both of the above options is that they will not be appropriate if your case is anything other than straightforward. By that we mean you do not know where your former partner is, or perhaps

they contest the divorce application making it a more complicated process than normal. If your divorce has an element of complication you would be wise to ask your lawyer to deal with the process for you. Otherwise you may find yourself unable to progress the divorce as quickly as possible. Talk to your lawyer at the outset and ask them to assess whether your case is one which they should deal with or one that you can process the paperwork yourself.

How much can you DIY when it comes to agreeing the children's arrangements?

It is not just divorce applications where clients are tending to take the lead. The concept of 'shared care' arrangements for children is far more common than it was 10 years ago. The reality is that the courts only make a handful of court orders confirming the shared care arrangements that are already in place. Many parents agree between themselves without ever involving the courts or even their lawyers in the negotiations. It is agreed when they separate where the children will live and how the day-to-day arrangements will be agreed.

Even for those cases where parents are unable to reach an agreement before instructing solicitors the way that the court process is structured encourages negotiation between you as parents rather than the Judges determining the final arrangements. Of course if you are unable to reach an agreement ultimately the Judges will make a decision locally. The judiciary are telling us lawyers that as a result of the promotion of Mediation they are seeing a reduction of up to one third of their case load. How much of this is motivated by parents looking to save costs versus the systemic changes that have been implemented is difficult to identify but the end result is that we as lawyers are seeing less contested children related cases than ever before.

What about the financial issues too?

If you are trying to resolve financial issues the DIY approach is not beyond you either. It really depends on how confident you are in firstly dealing with the assets and liabilities that you have and whether you believe that your former partner is being honest with you about what assets and liabilities that you have. Sitting down together at the kitchen table and agreeing 'who has what' has always happened but there has been a real increase in people trying to reach an agreement with minimal involvement of their lawyers in the past 10 years.

The end result for us as lawyers is that we tend to deal with far more people who have an agreement in place and want us to prepare the necessary paperwork for the court to approve the settlement than ever before. From time to time we lawyers may question the settlement that you have agreed if it appears a bit too one-sided or perhaps there are issues that have been overlooked. However, it is always pleasing to deal with a couple who have made a decision about how their financial issues will be agreed without the need for litigation. The biggest motivating force of late in couples reaching agreements has been the drive to save costs.

WHEN TO SPEND MONEY ON PROFESSIONAL HELP

What does this mean for your lawyer in terms of their role?

Firstly, your lawyer is still the main point of reference for all legal advice but the difference to their role compared to say 10 years ago is the fact that they will be dealing with far more clients who are compartmentalising their cases. The lawyers may be charged with sorting out the financial side of things but the clients are agreeing between themselves either with or without the assistance of a third party the arrangements for the children. The client will more than likely be apply for the divorce 'in person' and referring to their lawyer for advice if they are uncertain how to complete a specific part of the application process.

It is now mandatory for all people to have a mediation referral before making an application to the court for anything other than divorce. There are of course exceptions where it is not appropriate for a couple to mediate but that change in itself means that all lawyers now routinely deal with mediators. There will remain some cases where a referral to mediation is simply a 'hoop' that a clients jumps through before they issue their application at court. However, there are also more cases where clients see the benefits of mediation and use that as a method of resolving their disputes in favour of offer letters being traded between solicitors or an application being made to the court. Anecdotal evidence from the judiciary suggests that the number of cases being issued in court has reduced since the mediation hurdle was introduced. Whether this is due to the success of mediation or people choosing to settle their issues without court involvement as they have less money to pay for legal advice is too soon to tell.

How do you approach DIY?

Identify your strengths

Before you commit to take on responsibility for some or all aspects of your divorce, finances or children related dispute identify your strengths. Are you comfortable form-filling or is it the last thing you want to spend your evenings doing? Are you organised? If not, you need to be clear on the time scales for completing various forms before you fall foul of the court system. If you want to take on the task of your own divorce or children dispute proceedings, make sure you write down all the dates by when forms have to be completed.

Get organised

Make sure that you have plenty of blank copies to fill in before-hand so that you can present a clear copy to the court and if your handwriting is shocking, use one of the online packages so that you can have the form typed, or ask a friend who has better writing than you. Don't be tempted to do as the doctors do on your prescriptions! If the writing on your forms is not clear it will cost you time in delays and misunderstandings. If you are dealing with financial issues make sure you have copies of all documents you are sending to your former partner's lawyers or to other third parties such as mediators or financial advisors. Keep a careful note of what needs to go where and when so that you are not buried in requests for paperwork. Be systematic about looking through any documents sent to you. Are there any questions that you have arising out of that disclosure? If so, ask them sooner rather than later. Do you need to involve a specialist to prepare a report if you are talking about complicated financial issues such as pensions or life insurance cover. Do you fully understand how the various investments work?

WHEN TO SPEND MONEY ON PROFESSIONAL HELP

What additional help do you need?

Would it be sensible to ask a financial advisor to review with you the financial documents that you have and answer any questions at an early stage? It may be that worries you have about, say, affordability of mortgages if you both sold the family home and purchased two separate houses are unfounded.

Do you need to investigate the tax consequences if it is not possible for one of you to take on responsibility for the mortgage so instead the mortgage and family house remains in joint names for the time being but one of you moves out? When you sell the house in the future what Capital Gains Tax will need to be paid and how will that get factored into any agreement you have?

Are pensions going to be an issue? Do you need an Actuary to prepare a report to look at all the options available to you? If one of you works in the public sector and one of you in the private sector your pension provision could be vastly different, particularly if one of you still has a 'final salary' based pension. An actuarial report will cost money but if it presents the options to you clearly and you are then able to agree what percentage of a particular pension is transferred to the other person to provide a fair retirement income, is it money well spent?

Be realistic

Be realistic about what can be achieved if you and your former partner go to mediation. It is not the panacea to solve all problems. The good thing about mediation is that it encourages better communication between you, which is particularly helpful if you have children and want to continue to co-parent. However, if one of you is not a good listener or just plain angry then it will not be a great success! Maybe it is wiser to take things slower at the outset to allow the person who did not see the end of your relationship coming time to adjust?

Think about whether it is a cost effective option to involve a Family Consultant. Is one of you more emotionally vulnerable than the other. Would the overall process work better if the more vulnerable one of you had support? It is often said that separating from your partner is akin to bereavement. Having witnessed countless numbers of people dealing with their separation it is easy to see why this is true. As a family lawyer you get used to having a constant supply of tissues to hand and rarely does a couple separating present you with new emotional issues. The level of anger or emotional vulnerability changes from case to case but mostly it takes the person finding out that their relationship is ending at least 6 months to adjust to that concept.

Remember this is an emotional process

More often than not one of you will have been thinking about separating for a while before mentioning it to the other. The way that information is processed hugely affects how your case progresses. For some, there is a general acceptance that the relationship has run its course. For others, there is anger that the relationship is ending and not what they want. For others there is shock that it is happening and fears about where they will live and how they will cope with the change to both their lives and their children's lives.

In a way, it is easier to deal with those people who react angrily at first as more often than not, given enough time and space they will calm down. Sometimes, the early involvement of a family counsellor is helpful to as it enables those people who do feel angry and fearful for their future to have an outlet for those emotions and develop a

WHEN TO SPEND MONEY ON PROFESSIONAL HELP

strategy to move forwards. The expansion in the number of family counsellors available has, in part, been led by the move towards Collaborative law. One of the positives to the collaborative process which has been led by a number of practitioners in East Anglia is that we as lawyers communicate better with each other. We are more minded to involve family counsellors etc. as we have seen how they interact with our clients first hand. It is far easier to sell a concept to someone when you, as their lawyer, understand how it works and what the benefits to that person are going to be.

Make a list of those things you disagree about

If possible try to agree what you disagree on. That might sound like a bizarre comment to make but at least if you are agreed on say two thirds of this issues following your separation it means that you can instruct your lawyers to determine those outstanding issues only. This in itself saves time and costs. If, for example, you are both agreed that the family home is to be sold, and the mortgage repaid, and the equity divided in specific percentages but you cannot agree what will happen in terms of pension provision then you can ask your lawyers to advise you on the options. Of course you will pay for their time an expertise, and also possibly an Actuarial report if you want to transfer part of one pension fund to the other person, but far better to do that than say everything is 'off the table' and you start again.

Where you are agreed acknowledge that and make the money that you do have available to spend on lawyers work to your advantage! Much as you wouldn't necessarily employ a landscape gardener to mow your grass but you would to terrace a steep garden, use your lawyers and other professionals where you need expert help.

Be honest with your lawyer about your budget to pay them and anyone else

Don't be afraid of saying to your lawyer upfront that you have a budget of £x and you need to agree at the start where it is best to spend that money to get you the best outcome possible. An IFA can help you work out your mortgage capacity and explain whether or not you need to keep various policies running or whether it would be better to cash them in now. Mediators, if used, may charge less per hour than the lawyers to resolve disputes between you and your former partner.

If you are asking various third parties to get involved make sure your lawyer keeps a tight check on the expenses involved and agree with your former partner who is going to pay for which third party expense. Will they be shared equally or are you intending to use a particular 'pot' of money to pay for that expense. If you already have an IFA involved and you then ask an Actuary to prepare a report make sure that they speak to each other. Often there will be a crossover in the information they both need and by ensuring they both share information you may find the reports are prepared faster and answer the specific concerns you both have to better effect.

Where you are asking experts to prepare reports make sure your lawyer has a signed 'letter of authority' from you so that your Actuary, IFA etc. can contact the necessary organisations such as each individual pension company to obtain up to date valuations. Not only will this save time but it means they can get the information that they want to complete the task they have been set rather than the information you believe they want which is not always the same thing!

WHEN TO SPEND MONEY ON PROFESSIONAL HELP

So what bits is it best not to DIY?

As with many things there are some bits that are best left to the professionals. If money is tight and you are able to reach an agreement about finances between yourselves don't be tempted to think that you don't need to use a lawyer at all. You can apply for the divorce yourself, and you can reach an agreement yourselves but the court will require a properly drafted document in respect of the financial settlement which we would advise is prepared by a lawyer. If you do not have a court approved financial agreement you leave yourself open to further negotiations later on and more often than not that is not what is intended.

Most separating couples aim to have a 'clean break' meaning that they divide their assets and liabilities upon separation and after that they go their separate ways. They may have an agreement in place for how they support their children but the arrangements in place for the adults are final. This can only happen if the court approves a Consent Order. (A financial agreement drafted by lawyers and signed by both people involved which confirms that a deal is agreed).

Whilst you will have to pay for a lawyer to prepare this document, even if you do everything else yourself it is still money well spent. If everything is agreed it should not take your lawyer more than 3 hours for a straightforward deal to be put into writing, signed by both people involved and sealed by the court. The knowledge that your deal is 'watertight' is, in our opinion worth paying for. This is where you should prioritise your spending.

Now read the main points from Chapter 6 overleaf.

Main points from Chapter 6
When to Spend Money on Professional Help

1. With the advent of the internet, and the proliferation of information concerning divorce and the steps taken to commence divorce, it is now usual for those seeking divorce to take a number of actions themselves before incurring costs.

2. The more complicated your circumstances, the more you will need the help of lawyers in the early stages.

3. Many partners will agree among themselves child care and sharing arrangements without involving lawyers. This too saves time and money.

4. If you are trying to resolve financial issues, the DIY approach is not beyond you. However, this will depend on your level of confidence and co-operation with our partner.

5. Your lawyer is still your main point of reference for all legal advice, rather than "barrack room" lawyers. However, it is true to say that much more can be achieved yourself, thereby saving money.

CHAPTER 7

Children

How you sort out your children's arrangements now sets the footing for the future of the whole family.

Do your homework, communicate with clarity, avoid ambiguity and be prepared to be flexible. You then have a head start to making arrangements for your children work. Parents play a major role in promoting children's long-term adjustment to family change. Parents can protect children from the stress and anguish of separation by providing nurturing supportive and dependable relationships.

You may not be able to prevent your children from being upset, but you can support them and help them to adjust to and cope with major change in their lives.

Build good relationships with your children by spending time alone with them, being interested in their lives and activities, and showing them empathy and respect.

Reassure your children about the future, and reinforce the fact that the separation was not their fault. Look after yourself – you have to care for them so you need to be up to the job!

Communicate openly with your children. This doesn't mean providing them with all the lurid details, but be honest and open with them. Listen to them and try to put yourself in their place. Be available to them and encourage them to talk.

Try to manage the amount of change in their lives at any one time. If you can, make change gradual and give children time to prepare for it. Keep it positive when discussing change with the children, and try to give them time to get used to things.

Create a stable home environment. Have organised routines, clear rules and boundaries. Resolve the arrangements for the children as quickly as you can and support the children in their relationship with the other parent.

Whatever you do, don't use the children as pawns in a battle with the other parent.

The effects of children's ages

Babies – 2 years old

Under 2 years of age it is unlikely children will remember much, and they quickly settle into new routines. However, babies will pick up on tension, anxiety and arguments. Don't let then be aware of rows, give then lots of cuddles and reassurance. You will also need to bear in mind they will not grow up in a home with both parents and care must be taken to tell them why as soon as they are old enough.

Toddlers – 2 –5 years

Children in this age range understand what a fight is, they will understand some of the language used, and again they will pick up on a negative atmosphere.

However, with plenty of love and reassurance they soon settle into a new routine.

Schoolchildren aged 6-11

Let the children at this age have some reassurance that they are not losing you. They will worry that if one parents leaves, the other one may leave too.

Let your children's teachers know about the split so they can let you know if any problems manifest themselves at school.

Don't let your usual routines and boundaries slip because you feel the need to compensate the children for the fact that you have separated from the other parent.

Teenagers

Teenagers may appear like they're not bothered, but don't be fooled – they may well still be very upset by the separation.

Give them time to talk and stay interested and involved in their lives even if they try to stay 'cool' about things.

Take their views into account when sorting out the arrangements for them to spend time with each of you. Make it clear you are the parents and will make the decisions but you are dealing with young people who have valid opinions, and those views will be taken into account.

Teenagers still need affection and your support so let them know you're there for them.

Talking to your children

Make positive comments about the other parent. Your children aren't separating from your partner. They cannot change who their parents are.

Remember the subject of the other parent is going to be talked about between you and your children. Also remember that children listen to what you say about the other parent. It is so important they hear you talking nicely about the other parent.

So, find something positive to say because your children will love both parents, no matter how things have broken down between you.

Parental alienation

If one parent turns a child against the other, this is often called Parental Alienation Syndrome or PAS.

What is it? In essence it is where one parent persistently puts the other parent down to the children to the point when the children reject the denigrated parent and claim it is their own decision not to see that parent.

What your children want most is to be able to freely love both parents. Avoid saying things like 'you're just like your father/mother'. Hearing negative comments like this erodes the self- love a child has from both, and impacts on their self-esteem. An angry parent doesn't equate to a good parent. Children need both parents, so allow them that necessity in their life. Parents who really care about their children will endeavour to find a way to let children enjoy a relationship with the other parent without feeling caught in the middle of a battle between Mum and Dad. Ask yourself the following questions, and if you answer yes to any of them, then you should look at, and if necessary, moderate your behaviour.

Do I speak negatively or critically about the other parent an their family in front of the children or within their earshot?	Yes	No
Do I talk about legal matters, money or child support in front of the children?	Yes	No
Do I quiz the children about what they have done with the other parent?	Yes	No
Do I stop the children having phone calls, letters or gifts from the other parent ?	Yes	No
Do I impede the other parents' arrangements with the children by making my own which cross over or insisting mine take precedence?	Yes	No
Do I pressurise or encourage the children to take sides?	Yes	No
Do I ask the children if they love me more?	Yes	No
Do I let the children know I'm upset when they are with the other parent?	Yes	No
Do I prevent the children from expressing their feelings if I don't like what I hear?	Yes	No
Do I share my emotions with the children?	Yes	No

Telling the children

This is something many parents will say is the hardest thing they have ever had to do.

However, once the children have been told, they will often express some relief and acceptance because they probably knew something was up anyway! Parents should always remember, the children probably know more than parents think they do

Children are also sensitive to atmospheres between parents even if they haven't witnessed an argument.

So, if you have made the decision to separate, get on with it and tell the children. If you can do it together, so much the better. The children can hear it from you both, you can share the burden of the difficult task, and they can ask any questions of both of you.

Telling them together will also help to reinforce the message to the children that you both will be involved in their future and that you are fully supportive of the children spending time with both of you.

Make a plan. Discuss what you are going to say to the children. Keep it simple, do not apportion blame for the split and ensure you tell the children it's not their fault.

Tell the children as far as you can what is going to happen for example:

- Where you will all be living
- The arrangements for the time they spend with each of you
- Who is taking then to school (if there are any changes)

- When they will see the extended family (e.g. grandparents)
- If you are still in the process of making decisions then say so. Ensure you tell them you will tell them as soon as you know.

Answer their questions as far as you can but try to keep reasons for the split non-specific. For example Mum and Dad have decided 'we don't want to live together anymore'. Rather than 'your father/mother has left me and its all their fault'.

Try not to be angry or upset in front of the children, so work out how you will deal with this first.

Give the children time subsequently to talk about their feelings and ask any questions. Don't forget, this doesn't apply only to young children. Adult children can be devastated when their parents separate. Remember, for your children it will feel destabilizing, uncertain and distressing. We all have an image of a 'perfect' family living together harmoniously but life doesn't always work out like that.

However, the children can still have security stability, harmony and two loving and caring parents. It's just that they have two homes now instead of one.

Common questions children ask

- 'Why are you getting divorced?'
- 'Do you still love mummy/daddy?'
- 'Why did mummy/daddy leave?'

- 'If daddy/mummy lets me do it why can't you?'
- 'Do I have to like mummy/daddy's new partner?'

Use some of the excellent books currently available to help explain things to the children. A list of suggested titles can be found in the list of references at the end of the book.

Now read the main points from Chapter 7 overleaf.

Main points from Chapter 7
Children

1. How you sort out your children's arrangements now sets the footing for the future of the whole family.

2. You may not be able to prevent your children from being upset, but you can support them and help them adjust and cope with major change in their life.

3. Whatever you do, don't use the children as pawns in a battle with the other parent.

4. When talking to your children, always try to be positive. Your children are not separating from their parents. They can't change who their parents are.

5. Make a plan-discuss what you are going to say to the children.

CHAPTER 8

Parenting Plan

In this chapter we have devised a form of parenting plan we hope you will find useful. Utilise as much or as little as you wish. it will help the whole family to know what particular arrangements are and avoid last minute arguments. Try it and see. Consider using sticker charts for the children in conjunction with the parenting plan.

Keep a copy in both homes and let anyone else involved such as grandparents know what your arrangements are. Don't forget it can be amended if needs be. It is not a court order but a flexible working document with the intention of bringing some clarity to busy family life.

Sample Parenting Plan

We are:

MUM: _____

DAD: _____

CHILDREN:

Name _____ DOB/Age _____

Name _____ DOB/Age _____

Name _____ DOB/Age _____

Our Promise To Each Other And To Our Children

We respect each other as parents and we acknowledge the children's needs to enjoy a relationship with both of us.

We will both endeavour to foster and encourage these relationships.

We recognised our children's needs to feel loved by both of us.

We accept the need for cooperation between ourselves when making decisions concerning the children.

This plan is intended to provide clarity and stability for each of us and the children.

Signed (Mum) _____ Dated _____

Signed (Dad) _____ Dated _____

PARENTING PLAN

Emergency contact details

Dad   Mum

Home: _____   Home: _____

Work: _____   Work: _____

Mobile: _____   Mobile: _____

Children's Mobile Numbers/ other relatives / Friends:

Name: _____   Name: _____

Home: _____   Home: _____

Work: _____   Work: _____

Mobile: _____   Mobile: _____

Name: _____   Name: _____

Home: _____   Home: _____

Work: _____   Work: _____

Mobile: _____   Mobile: _____

MANAGING SEPARATION AND DIVORCE

School

_____

_____

_____

_____

_____

_____

_____

Clubs

_____

_____

_____

_____

_____

_____

GP / Hospital / Dentist / Optician

_____

_____

_____

_____

_____

_____

Living arrangements

You will need to work out when the children are going to be with each parent. Elements to take into account when developing a Parenting Plan.

Work / School / Nursery

- These elements are to a large extent non-negotiable. School times and terms are set well in advance (at the beginning of each academic year) and need to be worked round.

- School holiday timetables are usually available within a couple of weeks into each new school year. Make sure you both have one.

- The same is true for parents' working arrangements. If you are employed on a shift or agency basis, try asking your employer for as much advanced notice as possible of future shift patterns. Then provide the other parent with those details.

- Even if you work regular hours – i.e. the same every week, consider asking your employer if they can be flexible – for example by allowing you to finish or start early or to work flexi-time. Don't forget to tell the other parent if you are able to rearrange your working arrangements.

Children's activities

These vary from after school clubs to sports/dance/drama and so on. Write out a timetable for each child as this will help you to see where the activities slot into your parenting plan.

- Remember activities are important to the children. They will be thrilled that both parents have the opportunity to see what they have achieved.

- Don't use activities as a means of impeding the other parent. If football is every Saturday morning and the children spend alternate weekends with the each of you then either take it in turns to go to football or agree the same parent will do "the football run" every week.

Travel

- Who is collecting and returning the children?
- What times will be set down?
- Who is paying for the travel?
- Are car seats necessary and available?
- How will your handover take place and where will it take place?

Holidays

- Do changes need to be made to your usual routine to cover school holidays?
- Are you both taking the children away?

Childrens living arrangements:

_____

_____

_____

_____

_____

_____

Special days

For example:-

- Christmas
- Birthdays
- Mothers and Fathers Days
- Other special days for your family

All need to be considered in your plan.

Sometimes it is not easy to share special days such as Christmas. Consider an alternate year on year arrangement if it helps- for example if travel on Christmas Day is a problem.

Our arrangements for special days:

_____

_____

_____

_____

_____

_____

_____

Phone calls

Do you need to include in your Plan time for phone calls between the children and each parent?

You may need to consider more formal arrangements if telephone calls have proved problematic.

It is worth considering setting a day and time for phone calls as putting a structure to the arrangements can help to avoid misunderstandings.

Remember children don't always chat for long periods so consider a text message if they are old enough to use Skype if you have it.

Our arrangements for phone calls:

_____

_____

_____

_____

_____

_____

House rules in each parents home

It can be ok if these are different as long as clear boundaries are in place for the children and both they and you know what they are.

Consider:

- bed times
- Meal times
- Discipline
- Pet care
- Household tasks
- TV's in bedrooms
- Computer Access

House rules

Mum _____

_____

_____

_____

_____

_____

Dad _____

_____

_____

_____

_____

_____

Financial matters

Consider how you will cover the day-to-day costs of the children. So, who will pay for:-

Clothes – casual Holidays

- School uniforms Cost of holiday
- Sports equipment Spending Money
- Shoes Passports/Visas

School Medical

- Trips Dental Costs
- Lunches Optician costs

- After school / breakfast Clubs Prescription fees
- Travel to / from school
- After school care
- Nursery Fees
- Book and Stationery Fees

Who will manage the children's bank accounts?

_____

_____

_____

_____

_____

_____

PARENTING PLAN

Our financial arrangements for the children

_____

_____

_____

_____

_____

_____

_____

School / Education

- How are you both going to be involved in the children's education?
- Will you go to parents evenings / sports days / graduation ceremonies? Together?
- How will you discuss choices eg which school? which university? which exam choices? with each other, the school and your children?
- Will one of you ensure the other has a copy of the school reports?
- Who will tell the school any important changes?

Our decisions about education

_____

_____

_____

_____

_____

_____

Communication

- How are you going to communicate? Do you need to set a meeting with an agenda? If so, try to set up somewhere neutral, keep it business like and keep a record of what was agreed (minutes!)
- What are you going to do in the event of an emergency?
- How will you introduce new partners to the children (and to each other)?
- How will you manage disagreements?
- Are these decisions each of you can take without consulting the other first?
- What decisions must be taken jointly?

PARENTING PLAN

- If the children are away – e.g. a sleepover with friends – do we always need to tell each other where they are?
- What happens if one of us dies?
- How much notice do we need to provide if we wish to change arrangements?

Our communication plan

_____

_____

_____

_____

_____

_____

Now read the main points from Chapter 8 overleaf.

Main points from Chapter 8
Parenting plan

1. It is very useful indeed to put together a parenting plan. This provides a structure for the future. Keep a copy in both homes.

2. A parenting plan is not a court order but a flexible working document with the intention of bringing some clarity to future family life.

3. The plan will cover every element of life, ranging from access to children, living arrangements, financial matters, school and communications generally.

CHAPTER 9

Moving on

The rules early on

The decision to move forwards and establish a different type of relationship with your former partner is not easy and for some people it will continue to be a challenge many years after you have separated. They key to a successful transition from being partners to being able to communicate successfully as former partners is to try and get it right at the beginning. By that, we mean from an early stage try to avoid becoming involved in discussions that you know will end in arguments. Try to focus on the immediate needs that you each have, and your children have, rather than score points against the other person. Whilst it might feel good for the moment to 'have your say' it usually leads to further spats which more times than not severely damage the communication between separating couples.

All too often we meet people who have separated from their former partner and initially it is amicable and they intend to resolve their issues without the need for lawyers to be involved. Some achieve their aim but many others do not. It sounds a very common sense point to make but when couples separate one or both of them are highly likely to be hurt and angry. For some people this makes them less likely to be able to communicate effectively with their former partner. Others, especially where they are the person that has been thinking about ending the relationship for some time, are more pragmatic in their approach. Even then, it is important to acknowledge that whilst you may feel ok about your separation if your former partner is still trying to adjust you will have to give them time and space to get used to the new situation. There will be little chance of negotiating a long-term settlement on financial issues or the arrangements for the care of your children until the dust has settled.

How you handle yourself in the early weeks and months will go a long way towards impacting on firstly how much you spend on your lawyers, and secondly, how long your particular case will take to resolve. We have all heard of cases where one person is particularly vitriolic towards their former spouse leading to court hearing after court hearing taking place and the communication between them being non-existent.

As lawyers, we feel strongly that whilst there will always be couples that find themselves unable to communicate well it is imperative that we put the long-term needs of our clients first and focus on their long-term goals, such as being able to co-parent their children together, rather than scoring short-term points and 'getting one over' on the other party. A key part of this for you as the client is to feel comfortable with your chosen lawyer and, if possible, instruct a Resolution member. If a lawyer is a member of Resolution (formerly called the Solicitors Family Law Association) it means that they subscribe to the code of conduct ensuring that all family issues are dealt with in as non-confrontational way as possible.

Quite frankly, there is little point in you and your former partner agreeing to try your best to be calm and amicable if one of you then instructs the local 'pit bull' lawyer who threatens to 'shake things up'. When you instruct your lawyer meet with them and trust your gut instinct. If they are not willing to talk to you for a few minutes on the telephone before you make an appointment, consider how approachable they will be if you instruct them? Be clear about what they charge and how you will pay their bill. Also ask how accessible they are and how hands-on is their assistant.

Get help if you need it

All too often we as lawyers are faced with clients who are incredibly hurt or angry and spend a disproportionate amount of our time dealing with the emotional fall-out of a relationship breaking down. Whilst this is an inevitable part of our role as family lawyer we are not always best placed to offer the practical help that a person in this situation requires. Sometimes it is a simple thing like getting the support from your family and friends to enable you to move forwards and think about how you are going to live without your former partner being around 24/7.

There may be practical issues you need to address such as getting to grips with dealing with your own finances if the bills have been dealt with by your former partner whilst you were together. Suddenly finding that you have to renew your car insurance for the first time in 10 years can be daunting and this is by no means the most complex task you will find you have to deal with. The Money Advice Service Website is particularly useful in this regard and provides lots of practical help on how to organise your finances when there are significant changes in your life such as relationship breakdowns, children being born, retirement etc.

There is a greater acceptance of employing outside help to deal with the emotional issues following a relationship breakdown. There are many practicing lawyers throughout the country who now routinely meet with their client and at the first meeting they have with them a family counsellor or therapist. The idea being that the lawyer deals with the legal issues and the family counsellor or therapist deals with the emotional issues. We have had first hand experience of where this has worked successfully with clients. It can also be a more cost-effective way for a case to be run as if a person is particularly upset and hurt the family counsellor is vitally important in those early stages. Without their support and encouragement the client feels vulnerable. It is also pleasing to see that during the case the client, who started out being hurt, shocked and most of all sad, improves and starts to see that whilst their relationship with their former partner has changed there are positive things to look forward to. It is just that their future is going to be different to that which they had initially planned

If you have children together in our opinion it is even more important to sort the emotional issues out early rather than later on when one of you is increasingly bitter. You may be separating from your former partner but you are parents for the rest of your life. There will be events where you children would like you both to be present. If you don't handle this bit of your life right now it will impact for many years to come. Some clients find it helpful to focus on a long-term goal such as enabling communication to continue so that you are both able to attend your child's university graduation or wedding.

Don't just talk – listen too

The importance of listening to what your former partner is saying and trying to understand why they are saying it is often underestimated. For example, why is your former partner saying that they MUST remain living in the former family home? Is what they really mean that they want to ensure that the children stay within their current school and friendship groups? Is there any way that this can be accommodated whilst also ensuring that the family home could be sold to realise two properties being purchased? Or, are they scared of making the change if that home has been the family base for the entire length of your relationship? Change is scarier for some people than others, and if that change has been foisted upon you by a change of circumstances there could be resentment.

If what your former partner is saying makes you cross remember to take a deep breath, and if needed take a day or so to respond. (We as lawyers often do this when we receive correspondence from our colleagues that make us want to shout!) Making a decision when you are angry and cross rarely goes well! Take a day to calm down and you will deal with the issue far better.

Don't suddenly announce to your former partner that a major change is going to happen, for example, the money you give your former partner each month is suddenly going to be reduced by 50%. Think ahead to what the reaction is likely to be and plan ahead for their reaction. Is there any way that you can 'soften the blow' and have a transition between the current arrangements and what needs to happen next? Try to consider how you would react if you were the person receiving news. Might it be appropriate for you to signpost to your former partner that of the immediate issues to be resolved 'x' is, in your opinion, the most urgent issue to address. It may be a good idea to ask them to prioritise the immediate issues too as it will give you an indication of what you both need to sort first. It is highly likely that you will have different priorities!

Little people, little ears, long-term memories

Wherever possible remember that your children are just that. They are not mini-adults able to sympathise with your situation. In all likelihood they will be confused by why their parents are separating and probably fearful that they are in part to blame. Try to make it a golden rule that you do not discuss any areas of dispute in front of your children or when they are likely to hear those discussions. We recognise that this is a concept that it is easy to talk about but not so easy to do in practice.

Whilst it can be a good idea to put your thoughts into writing if you find it tricky to have a face-to-face discussion it can at times make a situation worse and not better. We have seen many cases where text messages or notes between former partners have been misconstrued. How many times have you received a message on your phone from someone where IT HAS BEEN TYPED IN CAPITALS? Is this simply that they are rubbish at text messaging and forgot it was being typed in capitals or were they sending a message intending to be 'shouted' at you.

Text messaging can be enormously helpful if you are clarifying one quick point about collection time of a child later that day but only where you are already on good terms with each other. Otherwise, steer well clear of texts, emails and letters and direct all communications either at mediation or via your solicitors. Paying for this at a time when you are both cross and angry can in the long run prove useful if it means that you are able to continue to communicate with your former partner long-term.

Beware of what you say online

Taking this a step further, beware of the ease with which you discuss your personal life online. Many people have Facebook accounts and other social networks that they frequently use. We are starting to see cases where the use of Facebook is causing problems. Whilst the Judges are not so 'hot' on the ins and outs of Facebook and the like, it can prove to be very damaging to your case if you have frequent 'status updates' where you are negative about your former partner and their treatment of the children, or where you bemoan your inevitable sale of the family home. A large number of children have their own Facebook accounts. If you and your child are 'linked' be even more cautious about what you say online. We encountered a case recently where a child was able to see their Father's status updates and he had been negative about Mum's attitude towards contact. Not good.

What about the children?

All too often we as lawyers ask the initial question of 'how are the children' and we are met with a response of 'they seem to be ok'. On the surface this may be so. However, the statistics tell us another story. For example, of the children than run away from home, a high percentage of them will be from a home when their parents have separated. Children's progress at school is frequently affected when their parents separate and some children behave in a way which they previously had never displayed. For example, your child becoming withdrawn or argumentative at school.

We as lawyers need to do more to ask you as the client what is important to you in terms of achieving stability for your children. You in turn need to help your lawyer by being clear about what you think your children need putting in place. As adults we know the reasons why the relationship has broken down but that information is not always communicated clearly to the children involved, leading them to speculate whether it was something that they did which caused the relationship to fail.

Many parents acknowledge to their children that separation from their former partner is an 'adult issue' and nothing to do with the way that a child has behaved. The children need to be aware of how things will change for them on a practical basis. Will they split their time between 2 homes and when will that take place? Will they still continue with their after-school activities and if so who will take them there and pay for them? What arrangements are going to be put in place to make sure that they always have school uniform and PE kit in the right place?

If possible sit with your children together and tell them of your decision to separate. Try to think of things from your child's point of view and address what you think will be their immediate concerns and be clear about how they will continue to see you both and where they will live in the short, medium and long term. If you don't know, it's ok to say that you don't know because there are some things that still need to be discussed. The discussion needs to be age appropriate and clear. Think about the language that you intend to use. It may be a good idea for you and your former partner to agree beforehand what you are going to say and possibly get outside help if there are issues you are concerned about.

Depending on the age of your children they may tell you then and there what their concerns are or they may become clear over the next few weeks and months. Inform your child's school and make sure that they are aware of the changes happening at home so that you can be informed if their behaviour changes. It may be that your child feels confident talking to their teacher about their concerns. If you already have a good relationship with the school it will ensure that the information comes to you as soon as possible.

Practical steps to take with the school

You will need to ask the school to amend their contact details so that copies of any letters, school reports and event notifications are sent to you both at your individual addresses. This might seem obvious but you would be surprised how many times we meet parents who have not received a copy of their child's school report and it then forms part of more resentment against their former partner where they feel they are ill-informed about their child's schooling. Schools are very used to dealing with parents who have separated and whilst you may find it upsetting to have this discussion with the school as it makes public the fact that you are separating it is a necessary discussion to have early on if you are going to be able to support your child.

Kids' turn and talking to you

Relate are trialing an initiative called 'Kids' Turn' which helps parents and the children navigate their way through divorce and separation. The course is run by fully qualified mediators and counsellors with the help of volunteers. The course is free of charge (this may change when the course is rolled out nationwide). The ideal is that both parents attend with their child so that you as parents understand more about how your child may be responding but you are given support to develop ways of communicating with each other so that you can co-parent. Children are put into age appropriate groups and given the practical support that they need both from their peers and fully qualified counsellors. The aim is to reduce the fear that children feel and reduce as much as possible their anxiety.

If the Relate-run course is not for you, maybe your children feel able to talk to their peers or perhaps grandparents about their concerns and fears. The first hurdle is to get the children to accept that they have concerns. The next step is to get the help they require whether that be more support from you as their parents or from outside agencies. We often find that initially the children react ok, but as the impact of their parents separating takes effect and the practical things start to change (like selling the family home or one parent moving out of the house) that is when the cracks start to show. Ensure that your children know they can talk to you when they are ready. In our busy lives it is easy to be distracted when having conversations with our children. Try to make sure that if your children do want to talk to you that they have your full attention, your mobile phone is on silent and you are not trying to cook the tea at the same time!

Key dates

Where possible agree at the outset what key dates are important to each of you. It is often said that you are a parent for life – not just until they are 18. It is also sadly true that you are unlikely to be able to continue the family traditions you both had when living together. Christmas holidays, summer getaways and birthday celebrations will evolve until you find you have begun new traditions. Remember though that whilst it is hard to think of 'missing out' on your child's Christmas Day experience one year, the same will be true for your former partner the following year. If you can have a consensus about how you will deal with the important dates in your family diaries at the outset it will save a lot of time, money and heartache later on. We lawyers know only too well the outcome of a contested Christmas contact case and although we can say to people at the outset that the court is likely to allocate alternate Christmases to you both, in all honesty by the time the cases reach us it is often too late to talk sense. Tempers have been risen and positions firmly adopted.

Review

Parents often say to their lawyers that they want to review the arrangements they have put in place for their children when a relationship ends and to see whether things need changing after the initial hiatus when one parents moves out of the family home. Of course this is important but it isn't the only review that is needed.

More often than not the receipt of a Decree Absolute can result in tears and although we as lawyers warn our clients that separating is an emotional process and there are ups and downs people seem often ill-prepared for the obvious. Another time when the reality of the separation hits home is if your former partner announces their intention to remarry or perhaps they are having a baby with their new partner. Whilst life moves on whether we want it to or not, the receipt of this information often sends even the most 'together' person to pieces. It is never too late to receive counselling. Sometimes those who have shunned the idea of counselling throughout the separation process turn to it at the end. It is almost as if it would have been a sign of weakness to admit they needed outside help during the legal proceedings but once they have reached an agreement and sorted the paperwork receiving outside help is more acceptable. If you find yourself feeling more 'wobbly' about the separation once matters are coming to an end keep in your head the idea that counselling is available and helpful.

Whilst paying for counselling in addition to any money spent on lawyers is probably going to be the last thing you really want to invest in it is just that – an investment. If you don't get yourself sorted – nobody else can do it for you!

Now read the main points from Chapter 9 overleaf.

MOVING ON

Main points from Chapter 9
Moving on

1. The decision to move forwards and establish a different type of relationship with your former partner is not easy and for some people it will continue to be a challenge many years after they have separated.

2. The key to a successful transition is to get it right at the beginning. This will also impact on how much you will eventually spend on lawyers.

3. If you have children together it is even more important to sort out the emotional issues early on.

4. Consider carefully your methods of communication and how you choose to communicate. Try to keep clear of sending texts or using social networking sites. Manage your communication successfully in order to limit any future problems.

CHAPTER 10

Resources

- Summary of expenditure
- Preparation questions
- Useful addresses
- Useful websites

Summary of expenditure

If you pay a one off annual fee, please insert what the monthly cost would be. For example, if you pay your TV Licence of £130.00 a year in one go, this would be inserted as a monthly cost of £10.83

MANAGING SEPARATION AND DIVORCE

Schedule of outgoings Item	Present Expense	Estimated Expense	Explanatory note if applicable
Personal Finance Costs			
Pension			
Private medical insurance			
Credit cards			
Loan repayments (not including car loan)			
Other financial payments			
Hire purchase			
TOTAL			

RESOURCES

Schedule of outgoings Item	Present Expense	Estimated Expense	Explanatory note if applicable
Housing Costs			
Mortgage			
Rent			
Ground rent			
Service charge			
Council tax			
Water rates			
Gas			
Oil			
Other fuels (e.g. wood)			
Electricity			
Telephone (land line)			
Telephone (mobile)			
Buildings insurance			
Contents insurance			
Repairs/maintenance			
Service contracts			
Maintenance of central heating			
Whole life policy premiums			
Endowment policy premiums			
Mortgage protection policy			
Appliance insurances			
TOTAL			

MANAGING SEPARATION AND DIVORCE

Schedule of outgoings Item	Present Expense	Estimated Expense	Explanatory note if applicable
Car maintenance			
Car insurance			
AA/RAC			
Petrol/diesel			
Servicing			
Repairs			
MOT			
Depreciation			
Car loan			
TOTAL			

Schedule of outgoings Item	Present Expense	Estimated Expense	Explanatory note if applicable
Domestic expenses			
Food and housekeeping			
Domestic help			
Window cleaning			
Gardner			
Garden plants, seeds etc.			
Pet food			
Vet Bills			
Animal insurance			
TOTAL			

RESOURCES

Schedule of outgoings Item	Present Expense	Estimated Expense	Explanatory note if applicable
Personal expenses			
Clothing			
Shoes			
Lunches at work			
Travelling to and from work			
Travel expenses not covered elsewhere			
Doctor/prescriptions			
Optician			
Personal toiletries			
Hairdressing			
Dentist			
Laundry/dry cleaning			
Beautician			
Other			
TV/cable rental/licence			
Magazines and newspapers			
Social entertainment			
Gym/other membership			
Holiday/weekends away			
Presents (Christmas and birthdays)			
Miscellaneous			
TOTAL			

Schedule of outgoings Item	Present Expense	Estimated Expense	Explanatory note if applicable
Replacement items			
Replacement household items			
Replacement furniture			
Tools for work			
Professional fees not paid by employer			
TOTAL			

Schedule of outgoings Item	Present Expense	Estimated Expense	Explanatory note if applicable
Maintenance liabilities			
Maintenance payments for ex-spouse			
Maintenance payments for children			
TOTAL			

RESOURCES

Schedule of outgoings Item	Present Expense	Estimated Expense	Explanatory note if applicable
Children			
School fees			
Nursery expenses			
Nanny/au pair/childminder			
Babysitter			
Travel to and from school			
School uniform			
School shoes			
Other clothing			
Sports equipment			
Sports activities			
Other out of school activities/expenses			
Equipment for above			
Nappies			
Toys			
Pocket money			
Books/magazines/stationery etc.			
Christmas and birthday expenses not included under 'presents' elsewhere'			
Gifts for birthday parties			
Presents 'from' the children			
Trips out e.g. cinema, zoo etc)			

MANAGING SEPARATION AND DIVORCE

Schedule of outgoings Item	Present Expense	Estimated Expense	Explanatory note if applicable
Extra lessons			
Clubs, subscriptions, fees etc			
School trips			
Holidays			
Holiday treats and outings			
Sweets etc			
Dentist			
Other			
TOTAL			

Schedule of outgoings Item	Present Expense	Estimated Expense	Explanatory note if applicable
Personal finance costs			
Housing costs			
Car expenses			
Domestic expenses			
Personal expenses			
Replacement items			
Maintenance			
Children			
TOTAL			

Useful information

The following are some of the more useful addresses and web sites.

Ashton KCJ Solicitors
Chequers House
77-81 Newmarket
Cambridge
CB5 8EU
01223 363111
elisabeth.sneade@ashtonkcj.co.uk

Asian Family Counselling Service
Suite 51
Windmill Place
2-4 Windmill Lane
Southall
Middlesex
UB2 4NJ
0208 571 3933

Association for Shared Parenting
0116 254 8453
www.sharedparenting.org.uk

Bilton Hammond LLP, Solicitors
Corner House
Union Street
Mansfield
NG18 1RD
01628 675800
diroome@biltonhammond.co.uk

MANAGING SEPARATION AND DIVORCE

Both Parents Forever
39 Cloonmore Avenue
Orpington
Kent BR6 9LE
01689 854343

Child Poverty Action Group
94 White lion Street
London N1 9PF
Tel: 020 7837 7979
www.cpag.org.uk

Child Support Agency
Enquiry line tel: 08457 133133
www.directgov.uk/csaapply

Family Law Consortium
Henrietta Street
London WC2E 8PS
Tel: 020 7420 5000
www.Lawyers-solicitors-uk.co.uk

Gingerbread
Single Parent Helpline 0808 802 0925
www.gingerbread.org.uk.
A support organisation for lone parents and their families, with around 20 centres in the country.

Legal Services Commission (Legal Help)
0845 345 4 345
www.legalservices.gov.uk

RESOURCES

National Family Mediation
Margaret Jackson Centre
Barnfield Hill
Exeter
Devon EX1 1SR
0300 4000 636
www.nfm.org.uk

Women's Aid
PO Box 391
Bristol BS9 7WS
National helpline: 0117 944 4411
Relate National Marriage Guidance Council
National Phoneline 0300 100 1234
www.relate.org.uk

Scottish Marriage Care
0845 271 2711
www.scottishmarriagecare.org
Resolution
Central Office
PO Box 302
Orpington
Kent
BR6 8QX
01689 820272
info@resolution.org.uk

Scottish Legal Aid Board
44 Drumsheugh Gardens
Edinburgh EH3 7SW
0131 226 7061

Scottish Women's Aid
132 Rose Street
Edinburgh EH2 3JD
0131 226 6606

Useful websites and further information-general

Useful websites

www.direct.gov.uk

www.justice.gov.uk/guidance/courts-and-tribunals/courts/family-division

www.resolution.org.uk

www.landregistry.gov.uk

www.moneyadviceservice.org.uk

www.relate.org.uk/kidsturn
0300 100 1234

www.ccflg.co.uk

www.iafl.org.uk

RESOURCES

Tax-contact your local tax office or go to *www.hmrc.gov.uk*

Pensions-contact the pension service on 0845 6060265 *www.dwp.gov.uk*

Social security benefits-contact the benefit enquiry line on 0800 220674 *www.nidirect.gov.uk*

Tax credits contact the tax Credits help line on 0345 300 3900 *www.direct.gov.uk/taxcredits*

Child Benefit- contact the child Benefit Help line on 08453021444

Preparation questions

These are questions that you need to ask yourself as you start on the process of divorce

- What do you want from your new life?
- What don't you want in your new life?
- What can you offer your spouse that they need?
- What do you need from your spouse?
- What do you need from your lawyers?
- Tell me what I need to know about how your family works?
- What matters most?
- Tell me what is really important to you?
- Tell me more
- Tell me about each child

- What do the children need us to put in place?
- Looking back from 2/5/10 years time, how you want to have coped with and handled this part of your life?
- When the children are in their 20s, and look back to this point in time onwards, what childhood memories do we want them to have?
- What's the worst we could do?
- What's the best we can do?

Recommended Reading

It's not your fault Koko Bear – a read together book for parents and young children during divorce by Vicky Lansky and Jane Prince. Meadowbrook Press.

Dinosaur's Divorce. A guide for changing families by Laurence Krasny Brown and Marc Brown. Littlebrown.

Clean Break by Jacqueline Wilson (age 9+) Yearling Books.

Helping Children Cope with Divorce (Overcoming common problems) by Rosemary Wells Sheldon Press.

Help your children cope with divorce – a relate guide by Paula Hall Vermillion Press.

Great answers to difficult questions about divorce. What children need to know by Fanny Cohen Herlem. Jessica Kingsley Books.

Putting children first; A handbook for separated parents by Karen and Nick Woodall. Piatkus Books.

Index

Accountants, 26, 33

Actuaries, 25, 28, 29, 34, 44

Alternative Dispute Resolution, 31

British Association for Counselling & Psychotherapy, 8

Capital Gains Tax, 57

car finances, 19

Child Support Agency, 110

Childcare, 18

Children, 63, 64, 65, 67, 68, 71, 75, 77, 93, 95, 107, 108, 114

Christmas, 19, 79, 96, 105, 107

collaboration, 2, 14

Consent Order, 61

credit cards, 19, 23

Decree Absolute, 97

Discipline, 81

Divorce Petition, 52

Domestic expenses, 20, 104, 108

emails, 92

Estate agents, 25

Facebook, 93

Family Consultant, 58

Family counsellors, 25, 30

Fear, 14

Finances, 17, 24

Financial advisors, 25

fixed-fee divorces, 52

General Practitioner, 32

grandparents, 4, 69, 73, 96

Greed, 13

Her Majesty's Court Service, 52

Holidays, 78, 82, 108

House rules, 81

Household bills, 20

Housing, 18, 20, 103, 108

Jealousy, 13

Kids' Turn, 95

Maintenance, 103, 106, 108

Managing Anger, 6

Marriage, 111

mediation, 2, 14, 30, 44, 45, 46, 47, 48, 50, 55, 57, 92

mortgage, 15, 17, 18, 19, 22, 23, 26, 28, 37, 57, 59, 60

Nursery, 76, 82, 107

Parental Alienation Syndrome, 66

PARENTING PLAN, 74

paying the bills, 17

pensions, 28, 29, 56, 57

Pet care, 81

Pride, 14

professional guidance, 3

psychologist, 4

Relate, 9, 95, 96

Resolution, 27, 43, 45, 50, 88

School, 75, 76, 77, 82, 83, 107, 108

school catchment area, 38

Separation, 1, 3, 1, 4, 14

Solicitors Family Law Association, 88

state benefits, 18, 23

tax credits, 18

Tax specialists, 26

Teenagers, 65, 66

texts, 92, 99

therapist, 4, 90

Travel, 78, 82, 105, 107

unsecured loans, 19, 23

Work, 14, 76

Other Information

Emerald Publishing
www.emeraldpublishing.co.uk
20 Newton Road
Lewes BN7 2SH

Other titles in the Emerald Series:

Law

Guide to Bankruptcy
Conducting Your Own Court case
Guide to Consumer law
Creating a Will
Guide to Family Law
Guide to Employment Law
Guide to European Union Law
Guide to Health and Safety Law
Guide to Criminal Law
Guide to Landlord and Tenant Law
Guide to the English Legal System
Guide to Housing Law
Guide to Marriage and Divorce
Guide to The Civil Partnerships Act
Guide to The Law of Contract

The Path to Justice
You and Your Legal Rights

Health

Guide to Combating Child Obesity
Asthma Begins at Home

Music

How to Survive and Succeed in the Music Industry

General

A Practical Guide to Obtaining probate
A Practical Guide to Residential Conveyancing
Writing The Perfect CV
Keeping Books and Accounts-A Small Business Guide
Business Start Up-A Guide for New Business
Finding Asperger Syndrome in the Family-A Book of Answers
Explaining Dementia and Alzheimers

For details of the above titles published by Emerald go to:
www.emeraldpublishing.co.uk